Wet Words:
Poetic Penetration
J. Visage

Black
MONEY

Get that bag!

Comfort Zone
She's nervous about her body when it's the same
curves that got me.
Like babe I undressed you mentally a long time
ago.
She said yeah but you never seen me.
Fuck that, I'm tryin' to rub you down and
release your body like a genie.
But she's shy though, worried I won't like what
I see.
Lifted her shirt like, "I won't lie though,
I'm inclined to agree. I don't like it I love it."
Followed her stretch marks to her oven,
to get her warmed up.
Scratches on my back, now I'm torn up.
And she ain't worried about shit.
Goddess energy, and I ain't hurryin' out shit.
I'm diggin' in her box for treasure til' I found it.
Punishing her kitty til' I'm grounded,
but I don't want to come outside anyway.
I want to be quarantined inside her for weeks
like Corona.
Internally springin' leaks like Ebola.
Got her body aching like swine-flu, no
vaccination.
Took her life and revived her no exaggeration.
Now she's comfortable as hell in my presence.

Shameless
You ain't got a thing to be ashamed of.
Gained a little weight but baby you can get the same love.
You'll always be a masterpiece, same one that attracted me.
Perfect is a state of mind.
Not something you have to be.
Kisses on your FUPA, tongue along your tiger stripes.
Skin a little looser, Imma hold you twice as tight.
I just want to see you smile again like you used to.
Every compliment I give, I'm really being truthful.
You just grew a baby and I think that shit is beautiful.
So Imma raise you up and hold you down like I usually do.
Hate to see you feelin' less, baby I can see you're stressed.
Lookin' at your face, I miss you facin' me when we undress.
'Cause you ain't got a thing to be ashamed of.
Gained a little weight but baby you can get the same love.
You'll always be a masterpiece, same one that attracted me.
Perfect is a state of mind.
Not something you have to be.
Attracted to you naturally, love how you do everything.

Even when you're mad at me, got me thinkin'
weddin' rings.
Still be sneakin' glances and double takes when
you pass me.
Take advantage of any chances to see them ass
cheeks.
You like it when I talk like that, I bite it you get
off like that.
And every time you ride, I get excited holdin'
onto that.
I'll support your choices if you want to get your
body back.
We can hit the gym together, eat better; I got
your back.
'Cause you ain't got a thing to be ashamed of.
Gained a little weight but baby you can get the
same love.
You'll always be a masterpiece, same one that
attracted me.
Perfect is a state of mind…
Not something you *have* to be.

Between the Lines

Would you ever make the first move?
'Cause I'm confused, don't make *me* choose.
If we never break the rules, I guess it's cool.
Just hate to lose…this opportunity, for you and
me, to be closer than we were yesterday…

Five Minutes

Don't have to wonder if you *came* like the rest
did.
I be puttin' you in chains, you're arrested.
Rise like the stock exchange, I'm invested.
Bite marks on your back, I'm an animal.
Eat the kitty like a snack, I'm a cannibal.
We get litty that's a fact like a candle do.
Leave you dizzy, it's like crack how I handle
you.

Sports Fuck

I talk a lot of shit, now it's time to back it up.
I got a lot of dick, now she's cryin' backin' up.
Handcuffed to the bed she's in trouble now.
Back shots blast off, got her duckin' down.
Said her last situation thought it was a race.
'Bout a run a marathon and pick up the pace.

Car Sex
She ain't never do it like that.
Take your shoes off baby, we can do it in the
back.
Push the front seats up, lay the rear seats back.
You don't need to get out, just climb the seats
and relax.
You must be used to me spendin'.
I'm fuckin' you tonight, it ain't no use in
pretendin.'
Usually be wining and dining,
tonight I'm pullin' panties to the side and we're
grindin.'
Got the windows fogged up,
Bendin' and balled up.
No religion, on my knees tryin' to tear your
walls up.

Rebirth
I'll breathe life into that pussy.
Mouth to mouth resuscitation.
Your lips against mine,
hands clutchin' on your waist and I'm patient.
I'm trying to taste it.
Get it all over my face.
If my beard is feelin' weird,
I can eat it from the rear.
Don't be scared,
I come prepared.
Boo this ain't for everybody.
Use my belt to tie you down and beat it up just
like karate.
We're discreet.
Don't tell the streets,
the way we freak between the sheets.
How you give me your soul to keep
When I go deep, put you to sleep.

V-spot

Spread your legs, Imma open you up.
Until the bed's wet, soakin' you up.
Givin' you head while I'm holdin' your butt.
Between your legs while I'm holdin' you up.
I love the way it tastes.
I aint even givin' dick yet.
I ain't even lickin' clit yet.
I aint pleased til' you're big wet.
Let me talk to it, tongue movin' all through it.
Two fingers, palm up, like I'm tryin' to call to it.
That's the way to hit the G-spot.
Kiss clit til' your knees knock.
Dildo and I'm hittin' all three spots.
Real slow, I'm who gets you off, he's not.
Tongue movin' up and down like a light switch.
Cum drippin' all around need the *pipe* fixed.
When I pull the tool out, it's excitement.
Oh I think she likes it.
Probably try to bite it.

Damage Control
We've been at it since quarter waters and chico
sticks.
I ain't playin, those silly rabbits can keep those
tricks.
You were there when I ran the streets, used to
free throw bricks.
No one can walk in your shoes, baby their feet
won't fit.
And if you let me, girl I'll give you the world
You pick the planet.
'Cause a real one would never take another real
one for granted.
You caught me when I fell,
promise never to let you fall.
Put a bandage on any kind of damage,
give you my all.

Fallen
I treat her well,
but she don't think that she deserves it.
Give her kisses, she gets nervous
I keep tellin' her she's worth it.
Heart is broken out of service.
Told her I would never hurt it.
Seen her ex hollerin' and cursin'.
Told her I am not that person.
I've been hurt too.
Why would I waste our time tryin' to hurt you?
You're always on my mind, but I know you got
shit to work through.
That's first boo, streamin' through comments
without commercials.
Just want a chance to show you *that* pain is not
universal.

Crazy Love
If I am not your type,
then what does it look like?
You could've been my wife.
I put that on my life.
Precious time is wastin' baby.
Runnin' out of patience.
Maybe I should let you go.
'Cause everybody says I may be crazy.
We've been together but not together, we're
more than friends.
It could be better, can't last forever it's sure to
end.
Texted you hours ago, and you left me on *seen*.
But when you hit me, I hit you soon as my
phone rings.
I tried to follow my head, but my heart took
control.
It's not a problem in bed, my part took your
soul.
And any time that you need me, you know I'm
running track.
Used to me rushin' to handle shit like a runnin'
back.
Got me thinkin' I don't deserve what I'm
looking for.
We hardly link, only reserved for what you book
me for.
Kind of selfish, you think that I'll always be
around.
But if it's you, I can't help it, I'll never let you
down.
You used to be my type.

But what would I look like,
Waitin' at the light?
We only get one life.
Precious time is wastin' baby.
Runnin' out of patience.
Maybe I should let you go.
'Cause everybody says I may be crazy.

Promises Fulfilled
Won't you spend a little time with a G.
Get in my ride, we can slide when you're free.
Take you all the places you ain't never see.
I'm on my job baby I can pay the fee.
Handcuffed to a lame, take the key.
He's too busy playin' games, lay with me.
Reservations all arranged, stay the week.
You're a prisoner of love, motive undiscovered.
Head in between your legs, got me under covers.
Have you screamin,' I'm feasting like it's the
last supper.
Heavy creamin' and breathin', I'll make that ass
stutter.

Proposition
I'm sayin' boo,
wont you pack a bag and stay a day or two?
He's makin' you mad, your situationship
debatable?
I'm about my cheese, girl I got it, let me pay for
you.
Got me on my knees, you're a goddess let me
pray to you.
We'll be overseas blowin' trees like the tornado
do.

The Plea

I'm sendin' hearts to all your texts,
We started off with sex.
But we ended up in love, because started with
respect.
I was focused on a check til' you walked by.
Almost broke my neck, took my breath, you
were on fire.
You get so upset when I jet, I'm a known flyer.
And I smoke the best, I confess, won't get no
higher.
You won't regret shit, kick it with me.
You'll own the best drip, fresh whips, no
gasoline, whip is electric.
Listen, I ain't playin' no games.
I'm not a dog, got some bodies.
I ain't sayin' no names.
We've been spendin' real time, got me layin'
some change.
You're my ride or die chick and I ain't changin'
no lanes.

Perfect
Say the word, we can take flight.
To the islands, we can dash on a late-night.
Tell the pilot not to crash, it's my eighth life.
I'm bitin' on that cat like a great white.
Blood in the water I still slaughter, I'm out of
order.
Park that ass on my lap, until we're out of
quarters.
But our time is never up.
Boo findin' you was luck and I'm tryin' to spend
my lifetime with you.
My super woman, I would fight crime with you.
Be your light up in the dark.
We're right up in the park, holdin' hands.
Picture perfect when we dance.
You were on my mind, so I wrote a poem about
you.
Too many takin' shortcuts, we took the long
route boo.
And I ain't even trip, 'cause I think you're the
shit.
And I want to spend my lifetime with you.
My super woman, I would fight crime with you.
Be your light up in the dark.
We're right up in the park, holdin' hands.
Picture perfect when we dance.
I'm kind of nervous but your kind is worth it.
That's why I'm tryin' to purchase you designer
purses.
But baby got her own bag.
A lot of days, latest hobby's phone tag.
I'm sorry that I missed you.

She hearted back, "I miss you, think I want to
spend my lifetime with you."
My super woman, I would fight crime with you.
Be your light up in the dark.
We're right up in the park, holdin' hands.
Picture perfect when we dance.

On Sight

Love could never be on sight.
That's like proposin' after just one night.
Nothin' could be *all* right.
I don't want to see the best of you.
I want to get to know the rest of you.
It's like a blessin' boo.
From conversations in your vestibule,
to long talks, long walks that's progression too.
I can't lie, I've been mentally undressin' you.
But I appreciate your dresses too.
All your effort and your essence too.
Girl your presence is incredible.
But will the present be forever too?
Was taught to never say never.
Hardly ever do.
Found the one now we're together…two.
But love could never be on sight, that's like
proposin' after just one night.
Nothin' could be *all* right.
I don't want to see the best of you.
I want to get to know the rest of you.

The Heist
She said, "Slowly, what's the rushin' for?
Hold me and console me, I've been lonely, let's
just touch some more."
Kissed her softly on the neck
Whispered-talk, "I know you're wet."
Put myself against her, she said, "Don't do that,
you know what's next…"
Lifted her off up her seat.
Missionary crossed her feet.
Pushed her legs behind her head, she told me I
was awfully deep.
Now she don't want me to stop.
I can see, she's 'bout to pop.
Streams turn into oceans, now she's soakin'
Use my mouth to mop.

Storms
Started with needin' me, now you blocked and deleted me.
It wasn't perfect, but I don't think you needed to cheat on me.
People give up to fast.
Can you expect for somethin' to last,
if we go through hard times, then you go and give up the ass?
Forget the past, all the good days, times that I made you laugh.
When it was lookin' bad, I hit the streets to try to make up the cash.
Couldn't give you everything, but I gave you all that I had.
Then you left, thinkin' the other side had greener grass.
I was open my heart was broken,
you made an impression.
So I closed it, felt hopeless, but baby thanks for the lesson.
No more stressin,' I took my pain, and it forced my progression.
Now I know that the rain and every storm is a blessin.'

King Me
Imma make your dreams come true.
Make a wish blow out the candles anything for
you.
Birkin bag matchin' sandals diamond rings for
two.
You're a queen, let me show you what a king
should do.
Imma make a way regardless.
Be the one to make it better when your days the
hardest
Baby let me take the wheel, get in my lane I got
us.
Imma lead when I have to. Follow when I need
to.
The only time I'm ever on my knees is to please
you.
The truth, so you get that. Cute that's a big fact.
And I'm addicted to the things you do with the
kit-kat.
Aint nobody better than you.
Total package, you're a savage and intelligent
too.
If you want it, you can have it, it's my pleasure
to do.
'Cause imma make your dreams come true.
Make a wish blow out the candles anything for
you.
Birkin bag matchin' sandals diamond rings for
two.
You're a queen, let me show you what a king
should do.

Ironic Platonic

In the bed or on the couch, get you wetter in a
drought.
Feelin' trapped up in your situation?
Imma let you out.
You've got doubts, you won't let me in.
You just want a friend.
That's cool, I'll make it rain until it's wet around
my chin.
If I kiss it, it's a wrap.
So exact, have you runnin' laps just to run it
back.
What I pack, proves the myth a fact.
She ain't goin' back.

Faded

Let's pack a bowl and get high, faded.
Now she's all in my ride naked.
Grabbin' all on her thigh, made it.
Drownin' all in her fire, taken.
Smoke with me and get lifted.
My rollin' speed is exquisite.
We're blowin' trees, we're twisted.
She's showin' me she's gifted.
She's too high for TV.
Pull two times, won't need three.
Blew two kinds, her knees weak.
Roll up again and get higher.
Too close to me, I'm excited.
Blow ghost, the weed is ignited.
Approachin' me, she can't fight it.

Fast Food

It's big facts, the world is like McDonald's,
Imma big Mac.
Model chicks lickin' my abdominals and six
pack.
Lot of women in the room wantin' me to hit that.
But if I kiss the pussy, you won't ever get your
clit back.
Big dick, last a long time and my stroke deadly.
Imma eat it first, then you better get your throat
ready.
Flood like New Orleans hurricane Katrina, broke
levee.
Swimmin' in your waters, I'm the captain and
my boat heavy.
Poetry like foreplay, I could do it all day.
Kissin' in the elevator, screwin' in the hallway.
Neighbors at the peephole, we're givin' them
free show.
They want to call the cops, but they're living
here illegal.
It's cool if they watch though.
I'm like an exhibitionist.
Crowd formed around us.
I ain't stoppin' let's just finish this.
Legs wrapped around my head, hand holdin' on
your throat.
Eye contact til' we bust, now let's go and smoke.

The Remedy
Thinkin' about your body on top of me,
ridin' me erotically.
Your eyes hypnotically guidin' me to your
privacy.
Lie with me, we'll play hide seek.
Hidin' but we play finders keep.
I'll give you that Vitamin D that will make your
body tweak.
I'm the doctor and doctor's orders are take a shot
of me.
You should let me hop in your waters my take
the yacht to sea.
I'm tryin' to make love, fuck, suck and impress
you.
Then recline, break buds, roll up and finesse
you.
You've been workin' all day, why the fuck
would I stress you.
Fed the kids, got them situated?
Let me undress you.
You're my superwoman baby.
Yes, you're definitely special.
Get the oil and relax.
Imma definitely stretch you.
Put your feet up, say less, then sit back on the
couch.
While I'm kissin' on your neck, Imma be
scratching your scalp.
Get in front of you on my knees, boo you
already know. Loaded gun, ready to squeeze if
you're ready to blow.

Deathstroke
Long dick, she's on her knees, I'm standin' up in back of her.
Strong dick made her start her period, I'm Dracula.
Flippin' her, you would think I'm workin' with a spatula.
Then she threw it back and started twerkin,' I was catchin' her
Fucked her on the floor, picked her up and hit the ceilin' fan.
She wants me to tailgate, forgot she was a Steelers fan.
Threw her on the bed, arms out with her ass up.
Pussy like a rose bush, she won't need the grass cut.
This was during Covid, I forgot to pull my mask up.
So if I die buried in some pussy, call it bad luck.
Premature ejaculation, I ain't never had one.
Hardly ever come from gettin' head, that's a drag huh?
Women tried and failed, I'm a champ, leave them disappointed.
Really wish I could, but I can't, they think it's annoyin.'
Type to make her come without no hands, like a burst pipe.
I just hope she that don't want a man, 'cause I'm the worst type.

The Recipe
Couple pounds of beef, that's about how much
the meat weighs.
Temperature is hot, cook at five hundred degrees
babe. Nothin' but an apron on, and I'm tryin' to
kiss the cook.
Put my head between her legs, like this is how
my kisses look.
Right hand on the bible but tonight it's on a
different book.
It's like fifty shades grey, the mission is to get
you hooked.
This is soul food; several pages take the pain
away.
Eighth inside a backwoods, lazy tryin' to fade
away.
She knows I like to eat; told me I should write a
cookbook.
I got the recipe I told her that might be a good
look.
Put some mood music on, preferably a slow jam.
This ain't Netflix, I'm about to change to the
program.
Really bout to go H.A.M.
but I don't need no pork though.
Serving only orgasms, I don't need a fork bro.
Two fingers and thick tongue, I can make you
say my name.
If you can make this dick cum, we're flyin' out
no paper planes.
Little bit of red wine.
We should hit the weed again; I forgot my next
line need the book to read again.

Oh that's right seasonin!'
Cover it and leave it in.
Let it marinate, fuck for two hours and breathe it
in.

Untitled

How do we say goodbye if we don't hang up the
phone?
If we both want to be together, why are we layin'
alone?
I'm sprayin' cologne, sit silent, just delayin' the
tone.
So excited to be invited, just a day in your home.
Just sayin,' I'm grown; I'm paying if you're
craving Patron.
It's wishful thinkin to be drinkin' sinkin' way in
your zone.
Patiently waitin' on my invitation, talkin' for
hours.
It turns me on, the way you seem immune to all
my powers.
Sweet dreams, liftin' you up against wall in the
shower.
Placin' you gently on the bed, your body
sprawled over flowers.
I imagine fits of compassion while we roll in the
deep
I'm hoggin' the sheets, slow kisses while we're
fallin' asleep.
Can't call it discreet, you next to me I call it
complete.
Music playin,' your favorite stations goin' all on
repeat.
Hold you tighter, my knees ticklin' the ball of
your feet.
Breathin' the scent of you, while heavy rain falls
in the street.

How to Eat

You're rentin' out your pussy to losers stuck in
collections,
Bad credit with their ex-girlfriends, little
erections.
They don't know how to eat pussy, you're
kiddin?'
I'm givin' lessons.
It's like tongue kissin.'
Suckin' and lick in different directions.
Put your tongue in it, twist it and flick it until
she's desperate.
Give her dick, then take it out.
Then put that shit back in again,
But you ain't fuckin' til' she cums inside your
mouth.
We play to win.
You ain't fuckin' til the walls inside your mouth
are caving in.
Til' your beard's wet and smells like pussy,
Doubt you shave again.
You gotta use your hands with your mouth, that's
the kill blow. Take two fingers, push them in and
out.
Fast then real slow.
And do it while her clit is in your mouth
Like a real pro.
Now it's time to fuck.

WYD

I just got the late text. Pulled up in some gray
sweats.
Hand around your throat from the back I like to
break necks.
And I hit it raw, since you're allergic to the
latex. Panties matched the bra, when I saw it, I
said say less.
Music in the background, fuckin' to the beat. I'm
blowin' your back out and suckin' on your feet.
We've been here before, fuck a couple times a
week.
Still sayin' I make you sore. You like it rough,
and I go deep.
Pussy like a ripe fruit, sittin' on my face.
Pushin,' I go right through, but this is not a race.
On couch cushions inside you, we're switchin'
up the pace.
Pull out? I really tried to, that shit was feelin'
great.

Turn-on Red
She told me all I want to talk about is sex.
I said "Yeah, but that's only after talkin' bout a
check. Now be quiet, let me put these hickeys on
your neck."
You were dry, now I got you drippin' on the bed.
You were tired, but I caught you slippin' want
some head?
Started grindin' when I put the tip in.
Hold your legs.
She said, "I'm trippin' 'cause the kitchen's
situation red..."
I said, "Baby, that's only hot sauce it's better
with it."
Put a towel on the bed, you can bet I did it.
Vampire life, sticky lil' thicker than water.
King size dick, make a long period shorter.
The last dude couldn't hack it, he was soft like
grits.
I go harder than some crack cooked with off-
white bricks.
And If there's blood in the water, wipe it off like
prints.

Tip Slip
We should take the kind of nap where our feet
touch in the bed
It don't have to lead to nothin'
Just keep touchin' the head.
I'm tryin' to rub all on that ass, "Lay your head
on my chest."
Have your leg over my thigh and feel the sweat
on your breasts.
TV playin,' hear what they're sayin' but the level
is less.
We were layin' under the blanket, now the bed is
mess.
Woke you up with black coffee, know my head
is the best.
How you're suckin' the black off me, I could
ever be stressed.
Really screamin' like we're in church, baby
heavily blessed.
Feel the semen about to burst, gravy let her
ingest.
Fallin' back to sleep?
Back shots wakin' you up.
Permission granted, givin' damage, but I'm
breakin' it up.
I can cum and clean it up, but that's just wastin'
a nut.
So I'm cummin' beatin' it up, puttin' my face in
your butt.

Booking & contact:

Blackmoneygtb@proton.me
Instagram.com/blackmoneygtbllc

Black
MONEY

Get that bag!

Wet Words:

Poetic Penetration
J. Visage